United States
Department of
Agriculture

Forest Service

Pacific Northwest
Research Station

General Technical
Report
PNW-GTR-843
May 2011

Camas Swale Research Natural Area:

Guidebook Supplement 42

Reid Schuller

Author

Reid Schuller is a plant ecologist, Western Stewardship Science Institute, P.O. Box 1173, Bend, OR 97709. The Pacific Northwest Research Station is publishing this guidebook as part of a continuing series of guidebooks on federal research natural areas begun in 1972.

Cover photo: Camas Swale Research Natural Area. Douglas-fir dominates the forest overstory with numerous shrubs mixing with poison oak in the forest understory. Hazelnut, salal, creeping snowberry, tall Oregongrape, baldhip rose, and oceanspray occur throughout the area. Photo by Reid Schuller.

Abstract

Schuller, Reid 2011. Camas Swale Research Natural Area: guidebook supplement 42. Gen. Tech. Rep. PNW-GTR-843. Portland, OR: U.S. Department of Agriculture, Forest Service, Pacific Northwest Research Station. 26 p.

This guidebook describes Camas Swale Research Natural Area, a 127-ha (314-ac) area that supports dry site, old-growth Douglas-fir (*Pseudotsuga menziesii*) forest. Major plant associations present within the area include the *Douglas-fir/salal/ western swordfern (Pseudotsuga menziesii/Gaultheria shallon/Polystichum munitum) plant association*, Douglas-fir/Oregongrape (*Pseudotsuga menziesii/ Berberis nervosa*) plant association, Douglas-fir/poison oak (*Pseudotsuga menzie-sii/Toxicodendron diversilobum*) plant association, and Douglas-fir/hazelnut-trailing snowberry/western swordfern (*Pseudotsuga menziesii/Corylus cornuta* var. *californica-Symphoricarpos mollis/Polystichum munitum*) plant association.

Keywords: Research natural area, Area of Critical Environmental Concern, old-growth Douglas-fir (*Pseudotsuga menziesii*), *Douglas-fir/salal/western swordfern (Pseudotsuga menziesii/Gaultheria shallon/Polystichum munitum) plant association*, Douglas-fir/Oregongrape (*Pseudotsuga menziesii/Berberis nervosa*) plant association, Douglas-fir/poison oak (*Pseudotsuga menziesii/ Toxicodendron diversilobum*) plant association, and Douglas-fir/hazelnut- trailing snowberry/ western swordfern (*Pseudotsuga menziesii/Corylus cornuta* var. *californica-Symphoricarpos mollis/Polystichum munitum*) plant association.

Preface

The research natural area (RNA) described in this supplement[1] is administered by the Eugene District, Bureau of Land Management (BLM), U.S. Department of the Interior.

Camas Swale RNA is part of a federal system[2] of natural areas established for research and educational purposes.[3] Of the 183 federal RNAs established in Oregon and Washington, 45 are described in *Federal Research Natural Areas in Oregon and Washington: a Guidebook for Scientists and Educators* (see footnote 1). This report is a supplement to the guidebook.

Each RNA is a site where elements[4] are protected or managed for scientific purposes and natural processes are allowed to dominate. Their main purposes are to provide:

- Baseline areas against which effects of human activities can be measured or compared.
- Sites for study of natural processes in undisturbed ecosystems.
- Gene pool preserves for all types of organisms, especially for those that are rare and endangered.

The guiding principle in managing RNAs is to maintain natural ecological processes or conditions for which the site is designated. Activities that impair scientific or educational values are not permitted within RNAs. Management practices necessary to maintain or restore ecosystems may be allowed.[5]

---

[1] Supplement No. 42 to Franklin, J.F.; Hall, F.C.; Dyrness, C.T.; Maser, C. 1972. Federal research natural areas in Oregon and Washington: a guidebook for scientists and educators. Portland, OR: U.S. Department of Agriculture, Forest Service, Pacific Northwest Forest and Range Experiment Station. 498 p.

[2] Six federal agencies cooperate in this program in the Pacific Northwest: U.S. Department of Agriculture, Forest Service; U.S. Department of Defense; U.S. Department of Energy; U.S. Department of the Interior, Bureau of Land Management, Fish and Wildlife Service, and National Park Service. In addition, the federal agencies cooperate with state agencies and private organizations in Oregon and Washington in the Pacific Northwest Interagency Natural Area Committee.

[3] Federal Committee on Ecological Reserves. 1977. A directory of the research natural areas on federal lands of the United States of America. Washington, DC: U.S. Department of Agriculture, Forest Service. [Irregular pagination].

[4] Elements are the basic units to be represented in a natural area system. An element may be an ecosystem, community, habitat, or organism. Taken from Dyrness, C.T.; Franklin, J.F.; Maser, C.; Cook, S.A.; Hall, J.D.; Faxon, G. 1975. Research natural area needs in the Pacific Northwest: a contribution to land-use planning. Gen. Tech. Rep. PNW-38. Portland, OR: U.S. Department of Agriculture, Forest Service, Pacific Northwest Forest and Range Experiment Station. 231 p.

[5] Wilson, T.M.; Schuller, R.; Holmes, R.; Pavola, C.; Fimbel, R.A.; McCain, C.N.; Gamon, J.G.; Speaks, P.; Seevers, J.I.; DeMeo, T.E.; Gibbons, S. 2009. Interagency strategy for the Pacific Northwest Natural Areas Network. Gen. Tech. Rep. PNW-GTR-798. Portland, OR: U.S. Department of Agriculture, Forest Service, Pacific Northwest Research Station. 33 p.

Federal RNAs provide a unique system of publicly owned and protected examples of relatively unmodified ecosystems where scientists can conduct research with minimal interference and reasonable assurance that investments in long-term studies will not be lost to logging, land development, or similar activities. Scientists and educators wishing to visit or use an RNA for scientific or educational purposes should contact the Eugene BLM district office manager in advance and provide information about research or educational objectives, sampling procedures, and other prospective activities. Research projects, educational visits, and collection of specimens from the RNA all require prior approval. There may be limitations on research or educational activities.

A scientist or educator wishing to use the RNA is obligated to:

- Obtain permission from the appropriate administering agency before using the area.
- Abide by the administering agency's regulations governing use, including specific limitations on the type of research, sampling methods, and other procedures.
- Inform the administering agency on progress of the research, published results, and disposition of collected materials.

The purpose of this approval process is to:

- Ensure that the ecological integrity and scientific and educational values of the tract are not compromised.
- Allow the agency to document research or educational use of the tract.
- Help promote the dissemination and use of information collected at the site.
- Avoid conflict between ongoing studies and activities.

Appropriate uses of RNAs are determined by the administering agency. Destructive analysis of vegetation is generally not allowed, nor are studies requiring extensive substrate modification such as extensive soil excavation. Collection of plant and animal specimens is generally restricted to voucher specimens or approved research activities. Under no circumstances may collecting significantly reduce species populations. Collecting must also be carried out in accordance with all other federal and state agency regulations.

Contents

Introduction

Camas Swale Research Natural Area (RNA) is a 127-ha (314-ac) area located in Lane County, Oregon (fig. 1). The site was established in 1984 as an RNA (Curtis 1986), and the designation was reaffirmed by the Eugene District Resource Management Plan (USDI BLM 1995). A short guidebook was written for the area in 1986 (Curtis 1986). Since that time, additional information has been compiled for the area, including a plant association guide for the northern Oregon Coast Range coniferous forests (McCain and Diaz 2002) and publication of the Oregon Natural Heritage Plan (ONHP 2003).

The primary rationale for designation of this site as an RNA is that it is a high-quality representation of dry-site Douglas-fir (*Pseudotsuga menziesii*)-western hemlock (*Tsuga heterophylla*) forest within the Willamette Valley foothills ecoregion (Dyrness et al. 1975) (see app. 1 for scientific and common names). This forest cover type is further defined within the 2003 Natural Heritage Plan (ONHP 2003) as:

- Douglas-fir/salal/swordfern forest
- Douglas-fir/Oregongrape forest

The RNA also contains a high-quality example of the Douglas-fir/oceanspray plant association, which is indicative of dry site conditions (Franklin and Dyrness 1988).

Recent forest classification work in the northern Oregon Coast Range and Willamette Valley provides an additional basis to enumerate the important plant associations[1] occurring within the RNA (McCain and Diaz 2002). These are discussed in the "Vegetation" section of this guidebook.

---

[1] Plant associations are named based on a combination of the dominant life form plus the characteristic or dominant plant species in the various plant layers (trees, shrubs, and herbs). Plant association acronyms are a shorthand form for communicating the plant association name. Each acronym is made up of the first two letters of the genus name of the dominant or characteristic species within a layer, and combined with the first two letters of the specific epithet of the species (e.g., *Pseudotsuga menziesii* is shortened to PSME). Plant associations are generally defined by the dominant or characteristic species that occupies the uppermost vegetation layer. In forested plant associations, this is the tree layer. Additional names are used for understory layers when they contain dominant, characteristic, or diagnostic species (e.g., *Pseudotsuga menziesii/Corylus cornuta* var. *californica-Symphoricarpos mollis/Polystichum munitum*) = PSME/COCOC-SYMO/POMU. Life form layers are separated by "/". Co-dominants within a layer are separated by "-". The association may have only one species in its name (e.g., the herb layer in meadows), two where shrubs are superimposed over the herbaceous layer, or three where there are tree, shrub, and herb layers (Kovalchik and Clausnitzer 2004).

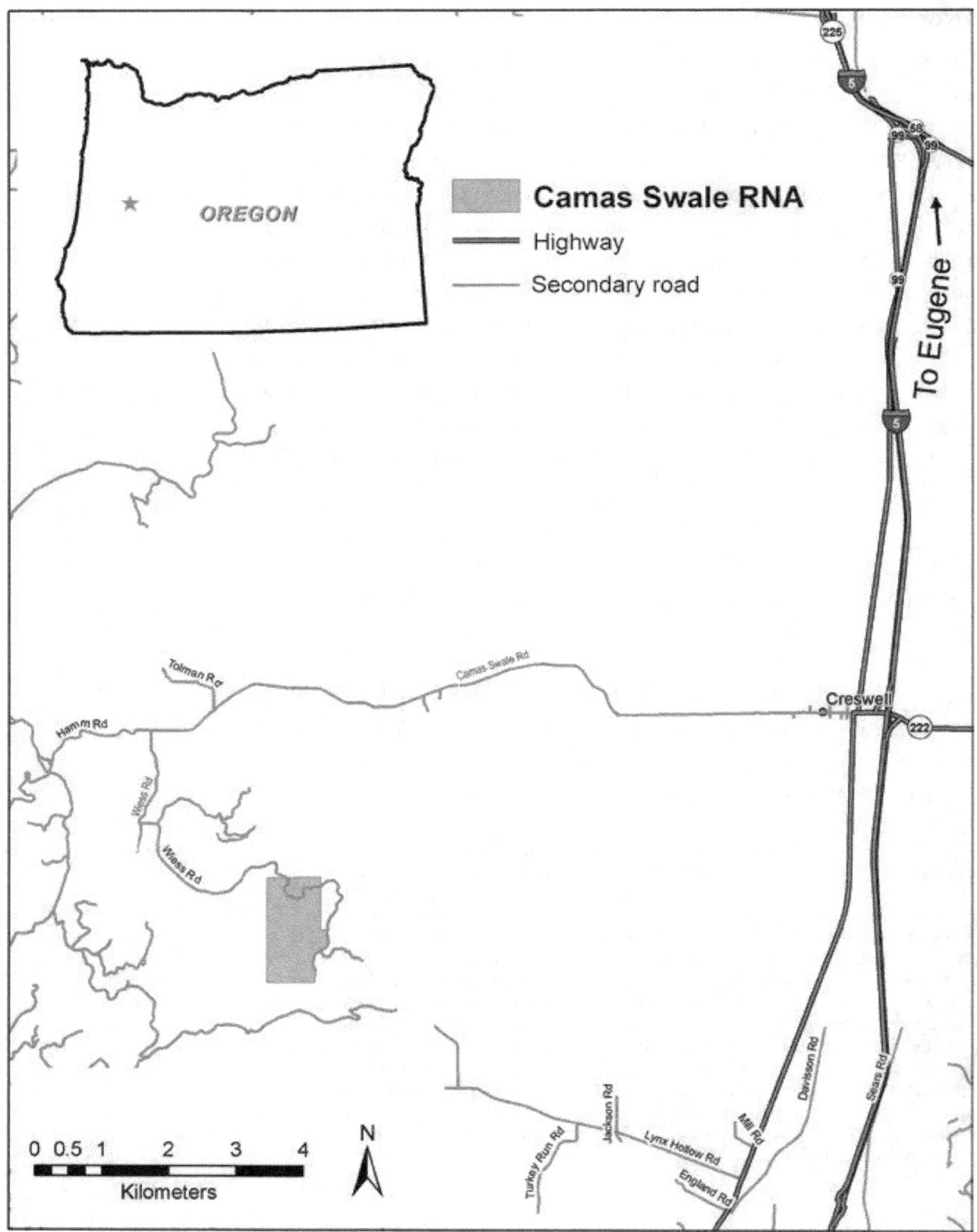

Figure 1—Camas Swale Research Natural Area (RNA) location and access.

Access and Accommodations

The RNA is located in Section 25, Township 19 South, R 4 West, Willamette Meridian, in Lane County, Oregon. To access the area from Interstate 5 in Creswell, Oregon (18 km [11 mi] south of Eugene, Oregon), proceed west from Interstate 5, through Creswell, for 12 km (7.3 mi) on Camas Swale Road. Turn left (south) onto Weiss Road and follow it for 3 km (2 mi) to its intersection with Bureau of Land Management (BLM) road 19-4-26 to a locked gate (a key must be obtained from the BLM office in Springfield to gain entry beyond this point). Follow the road through the gate for 1 km (0.7 mi) to the northern boundary of the RNA (fig. 1).

Prior to visiting the site, obtain permission to access the area for research or educational purposes at the BLM, Eugene District office in Springfield, Oregon. Maps and additional directions to the area are available at the Eugene District office.

The purposes of the approval process for research and monitoring on RNAs are:

- To ensure that the ecological integrity of the RNA or other purposes for which the RNA was designated are not damaged by research or related activities.
- To provide information to scientists about other research occurring on the RNA so that potential collaborations may be fostered and conflicts avoided.
- To ensure that protection and site integrity for the individual scientific study, especially permanent plots, are maintained.
- To maintain records of research activities and research results to benefit the BLM, other agencies, and future researchers (Wilson et al. 2009).

Lodging is available in Eugene, Springfield, Cottage Grove, and Creswell, Oregon.

Environment

The RNA is situated within low, rolling foothills along the boundary of the Willamette Valley and Coast Range physiographic provinces (ONHP 2003, USDI BLM 1982). Elevations range from 244 m (800 ft) in the northwest portion of the tract to 408 m (1,340 ft) near the southeastern boundary. Slopes are moderately inclined and drainage of seasonal creeks is to the west (table 1). A full range of slope exposures occur within the tract (fig. 2).

Geologically, the RNA is mapped as Eocene age Fisher Formation composed of nonmarine water-deposited tuffs and conglomerates. Soils in the general area formed in colluvium and residuum derived from sandstone, siltstone, volcanic tuff, or basic igneous rock. The area is mapped as the Bellpine soil series and the Dixonville Philomath-Hazelair soil complex (USDA NRCS 2010). These soils

Table 1—Physiographic attributes of four permanent plots, Camas Swale Research Natural Area

	Plot			
	1	2	3	4
Elevation (m)	311	314	366	372
Aspect (°)	196	140	277	178
Slope grade (%)	20	33	25	28
Slope position	Upper 1/3	Upper 1/3	Upper 1/3	Upper 1/3

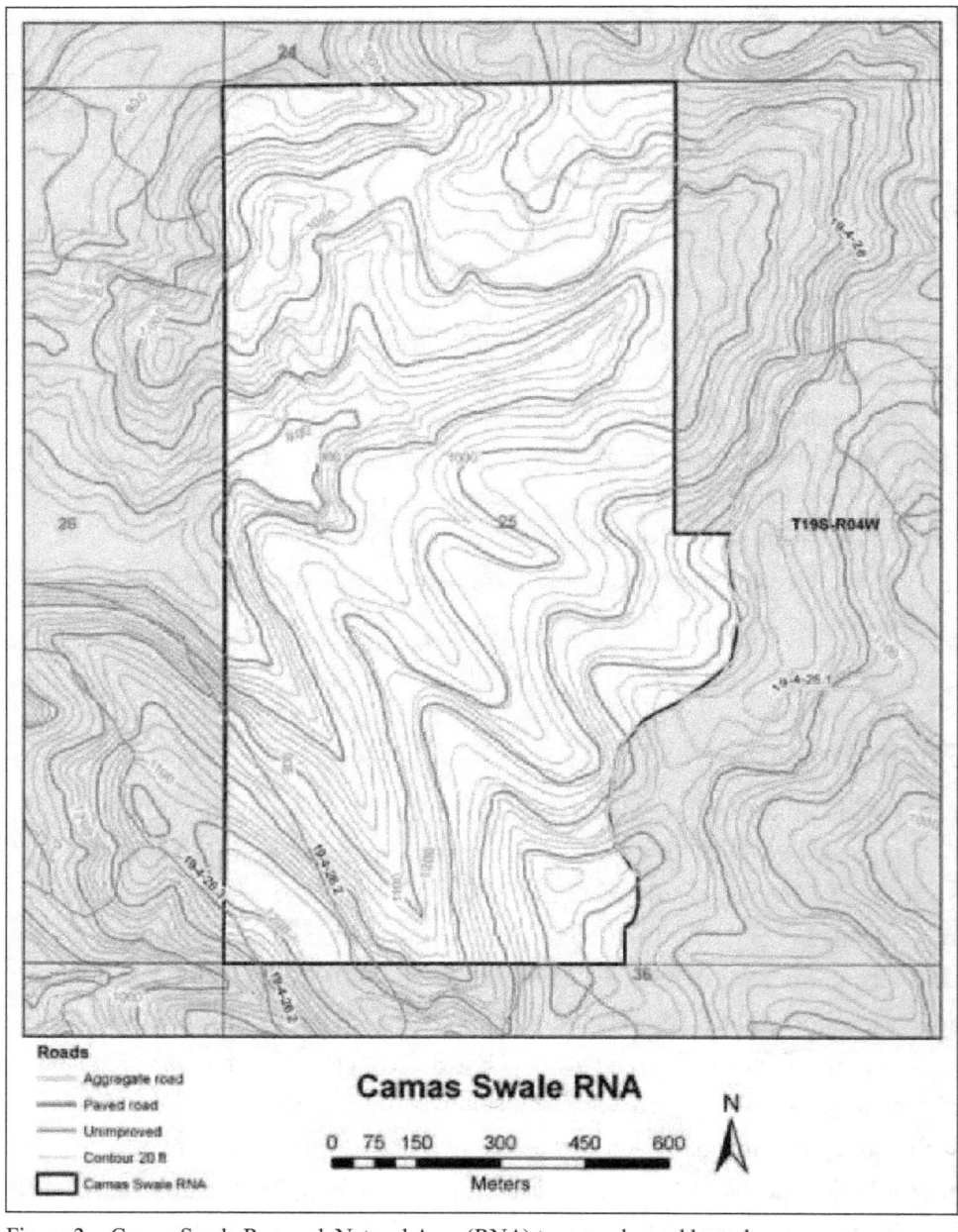

Figure 2—Camas Swale Research Natural Area (RNA) topography and boundary.

occur on nearly level to steep, moderately deep to shallow, well-drained and moderately well-drained soils on foothills adjacent to the Willamette Valley. They include silty clay loam, cobbly silty clay loam, and cobbly silty clay. These soils range in depth from 20 to 40 inches (51 to 102 cm). Included in the RNA are Ritner and Witzel soils with Rock Outcrop (Baitis 2010). Witzel soils are very shallow—30 to 51 cm (12 to 20 inches)—and the rock outcrops are composed of basic igneous rock overlain by a thin soil mantle that has a very low available water capacity with rapid runoff. Rock outcrops are very droughty and frequently do not support tree growth (Patching 1987).

Three intermittent first- and second-order streams occur in west-facing ravines and periodically contain surface water.

Climate

The climate is mediterranean and is characterized by hot, dry summer and cool, wet winters. From late fall through spring, unstable low-pressure air masses bring frequent storms accompanied by high winds from the Pacific Ocean. During the summer, stable high-pressure air masses bring generally clear skies and temperature inversions. Proximity of the area to the Pacific Ocean mitigates temperature extremes (USDI BLM 1982).

The weather station nearest to the RNA is the Eugene Airport, Oregon (352709) weather station, which is located about 32 km (20 mi) to the northwest of the RNA at a comparable elevation. Extended periods of cloudiness and heavy periods of precipitation occur during the winter. Precipitation occurs primarily as rain and averages 1145 mm (45.06 in) per year. Approximately 70 percent of average annual precipitation falls from November through March. Five percent of the average annual precipitation occurs during the June through August period (Curtis 1986, WRCC 2010). Additional climate parameters are summarized in table 2.

Table 2—Temperature and precipitation summary 12/1/1939 to 12/31/2009, Eugene Airport, Oregon (352709)

Average minimum January temperature	0.8 °C (33.5 °F)
Average maximum January temperature	7.9 °C (46.3 °F)
Average minimum July temperature	10.8 °C (51.4 °F)
Average maximum July temperature	28.0 °C (82.4 °F)
Average annual precipitation	1145 mm (45.06 in)
Average June-August precipitation	63 mm (2.47 in)
Average annual snowfall	152 mm (6.0 in)

Vegetation

Douglas-fir (*Pseudotsuga menziesii*) is the dominant upper canopy tree throughout the natural area. Large specimens of Douglas-fir occur throughout except for the northwest portion of the tract (fig. 3). Large individual incense cedar (*Calocedrus decurrens*) and ponderosa pine (*Pinus ponderosa*) are scattered throughout the site (Curtis 1986). Unlike adjacent Coast Range forest, western hemlock and western redcedar (*Thuja plicata*) are absent (USDI BLM 1982). Long-term monitoring plots were established in 2001 and remeasured in 2009 to quantify change in forest stand structure and composition over time (Schuller and Greene 2009, Schuller et al. 2001). Based on 15 tree cores taken in 2001, the majority of Douglas-firs were established between 1853 and 1863. In 2009, these trees averaged 49 cm (19 in) d.b.h.[2] Larger Douglas-fir >100 cm (39 in) are also present in the area and are estimated to be more than 300 years old.

Old-growth Douglas-fir forest

Forest understory tree regeneration is sparse and is composed of Douglas-fir with grand fir (*Abies grandis*) present on mesic sites. Giant chinquapin (*Chrysolepis chrysophylla)* occurs in canopy openings and along margins of the xeric meadow with Oregon white oak (*Quercus garryana*).

Understory shrub cover is highly variable and ranges between 10 and 70 percent (table 3). Major shrubs include hazelnut (*Corylus cornuta* var. *californica*), poison oak (*Toxicodendron diversilobum*), oceanspray (*Holodiscus discolor*), and vine maple (*Acer circinatum*). Numerous other shrubs and vines occur in minor amounts including baldhip rose (*Rosa gymnocarpa*), salal (*Gaultheria shallon*), tall Oregongrape (*Berberis aquifolium*), Oregongrape (*Berberis nervosa*), pink honeysuckle (*Lonicera hispidula*), and creeping snowberry (*Symphoricarpos mollis*).

Herbaceous vegetation is characterized by western swordfern (*Polystichum munitum*), American trailplant (*Adenocaulon bicolor*), and sweetcicely (*Osmorhiza berteroi*). Other occasional understory plants include twinflower (*Linnaea borealis*), snowqueen (*Synthyris reniformis*), California harebell (*Campanula prenanthoides*), and sweet-scented bedstraw (*Galium triflorum*). Grasses occur frequently, but at low coverage values. Typical species are western fescue (*Festuca occidentalis*), bearded fescue (*Festuca subulata*), Alaska oniongrass (*Melica subulata*), common brome (*Bromus vulgaris*), and soft brome (*B. hordeaceus*) (table 3).

Xeric meadow

A 2.4-ha (5.9-ac) xeric meadow and fringing Oregon white oak woodland occurs in the northwest portion of the tract on very shallow soils (fig. 3). The

---

[2] "D.b h." refers to diameter at breast height, a measurement taken at 1.47 m above the ground.

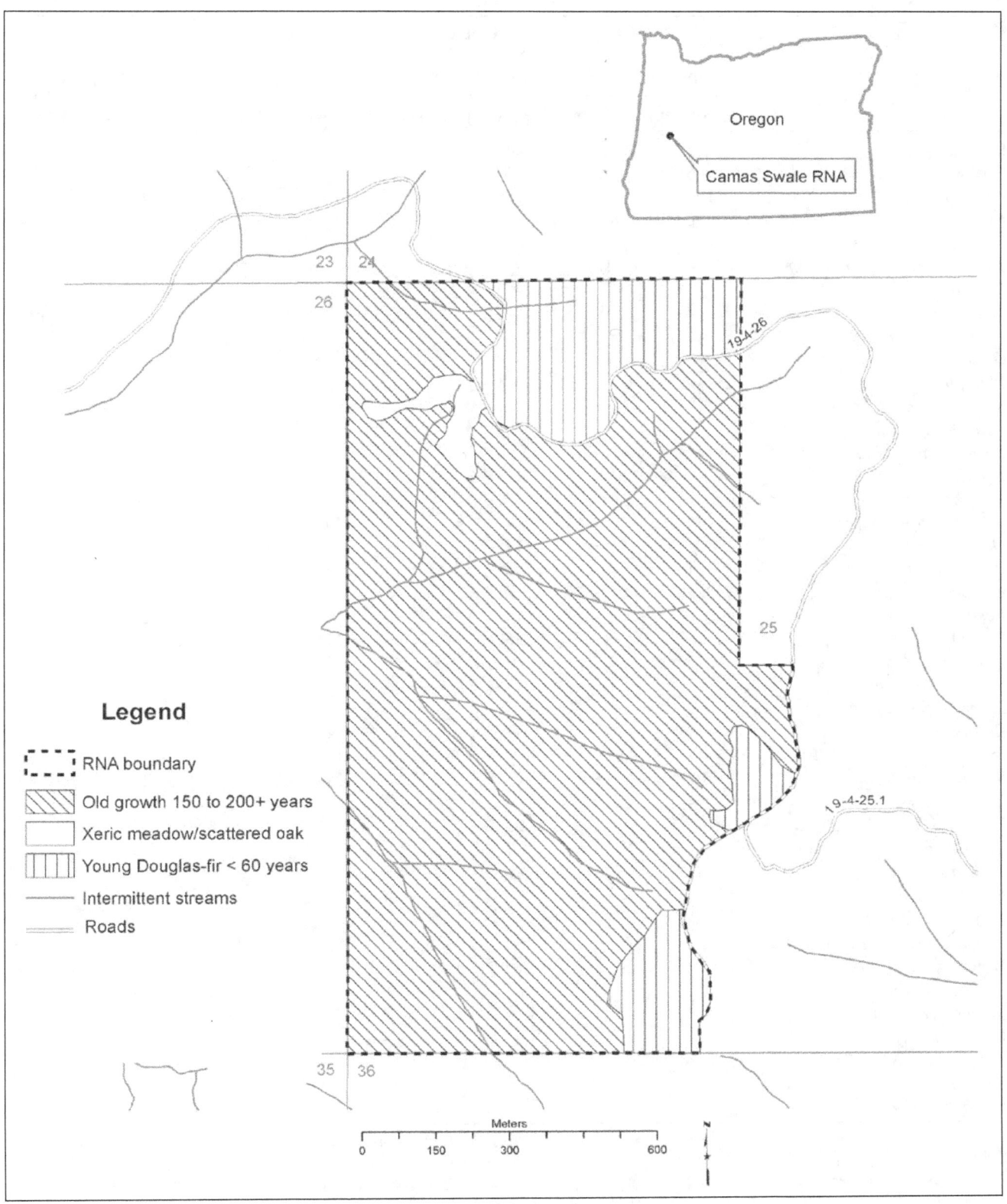

Figure 3—Camas Swale Research Natural Area (RNA) vegetation and hydrology.

Table 3—Plant association, understory coverage, and frequency of four permanent plots in Camas Swale Research Natural Area

	Plot 1 PSME/TODI[a]		Plot 2 PSME/TODI		Plot 3 PSME/TODI		Plot 4 PSME/COCOC-SYMO/POMU	
	Frequency[b]	Cover	Frequency	Cover	Frequency	Cover	Frequency	Cover
Bare ground	7	+	4	+	4	1		
Coarse litter	46	6	36	11	64	12	39	11
Fine litter	100	90	100	98	100	94	100	96
Moss	96	60	93	69	100	76	93	46
Corylus cornuta var. *californica*[c]	—	1	—	24	—	22	—	70
Toxicodendron diversilobum	—	10	—	17	—	17	—	2
Holodiscus discolor	—		—	15	—	6	—	3
Acer circinatum	—		—		—		—	49
Rosa gymnocarpa	—		—	+	—		—	1
Gaultheria shallon	—		—	1	—		—	3
Whipplea modesta	—		—	1	—		—	2
Rubus ursinus	—	+	—	+	—	2	—	+
Lonicera hispidula	—	1	—	+	—		—	+
Berberis aquifolium								
Berberis nervosa[d]	—	6	—	2	—		—	
Symphoricarpos mollis	—		—	+	—	+	—	
Adenocaulon bicolor	39	3	4	+	46	3	18	1
Osmorhiza berteroi	25	+	14	1	46	4	4	+
Polystichum munitum	21	10	43	30	4	+	18	8
Anisocarpus madioides	21	1	4	+				
Festuca occidentalis	7	+	14	+	18	+	21	+
Galium triflorum	25	1	25	1	29	+	39	+
Festuca subulata	25	+	7	+	7	+	29	+
Linnaea borealis	21	+	7	+	43	4	7	+
Lathyrus pauciflorus	4	+	4	+				
Bromus hordeaceus	18	+	11	+	14	+		
Iris tenax	11	+			11	+		
Synthyris reniformis	4	+	25	1	21	1	29	2
Nemophila parviflora	4	+						
Trientalis borealis ssp. *latifolia*			25	1	14	1	25	1
Campanula prenanthoides			7	+	32	2	39	1
Melica subulata					71	2		
Fragaria vesca					14	+	11	+
Cynoglossum grande					7	1		
Cardamine nuttallii var. *nuttallii*					7	+		
Vancouveria hexandra					4	+	4	+
Viola sempervirens							14	+
Anemone deltoidea							14	+
Iris chrysophylla							7	+
Sanicula crassicaulis							7	+
Satureja douglasii							7	+
Stachys rigida							4	+

[a] PSME = *Pseudotsuga menziesii*, TODI = *Toxicodendron diversilobum*, COCOC = *Corylus cornuta* var. *californica*, SYMO = *Symphoricarpos mollis*, POMU = *Polystichum munitum*, + = trace (<0.5 percent foliar cover); — = not recorded.

[b] Cover is expressed as percentage of foliar cover; frequency is expressed as percentage of relative frequency. Zero values are not included.

[c] See appendix 1 for a listing of scientific and common names.

[d] McCain and Diaz (2002) refer to *Berberis nervosa* as *Mahonia nervosa*. The currently accepted name of *Berberis nervosa* is used in this document. See: Flora of North America (1993+) and the Oregon Flora Project (2010) in the "References" section.

meadow is dominated by bristly dogstail grass (*Cynosurus echinatus*), an invasive nonnative species. Numerous native herbaceous species also occur in the meadow, including common yarrow (*Achillea millefolium)*, common monkeyflower (*Mimulus guttatus*), self-heal (*Prunella vulgaris*), and Oregon saxifrage (*Saxifraga oregana*). Douglas-fir is invading this area owing to the absence of recent fire (fig. 4).

Four, 1000-m^2 circular plots were established in 2001 (Schuller et al. 2001) and remeasured in 2009 (Schuller and Greene 2009) to monitor change in vegetation structure and composition over time (table 3). Data were used to classify plot vegetation into forest plant associations. Figure 5 shows typical stand conditions within the Douglas-fir/poison oak (*Pseudotsuga menziesii/Toxicodendron diversilobum*) plant association, where numerous medium to tall shrubs co-mingle with poison oak in the forest understory. One plot exemplifies the Douglas-fir/hazelnut-creeping snowberry/western swordfern (*Pseudotsuga menziesii/Corylus cornuta* var. *californica-Symphoricarpos mollis/Polystichum munitum*) plant association, where medium and tall shrubs predominate, but with only minor coverage of poison oak on the forest floor (fig. 6) (table 2).

A full list of scientific and common names for vascular plants known to occur in the RNA is provided in appendix 1.

Reid Schuller

Figure 4—Meadow invasion by Douglas-fir: a sign of the absence of recent fire in the area.

Figure 5—Poison oak is a major understory component within the Douglas-fir/poison oak plant association. Poison oak grows both as an understory herb and as a vine on Douglas-fir.

Figure 6—Understory conditions within the Douglas-fir/hazelnut-creeping snowberry/western swordfern plant association. Shrubs dominate the understory, with only minor coverage of poison oak.

Fauna

Amphibians, reptiles, birds, and mammals known or expected to occur within the RNA are listed in appendix 2. These lists have been derived from field observation (Curtis 1986, Maser 1973) and published literature (Csuti et al. 1997).

Disturbance History

Recent geographic information system mapping and re-creation of historical vegetation patterns in the Willamette Valley during the 1850s suggest that the RNA was mostly closed forest, but also included woodland (defined as 25 to 60 percent cover) based on General Land Office data (Christy et al. 2009).

Since that time, at least one major forest fire occurred in the area, as evidenced by the deep scars burned into trunks of nearly all old-growth incense cedars. This fire contributed to Douglas-fir continuing to maintain its dominance in the area. No fires have been reported since fire suppression was initiated in the area during the 1930s (Curtis 1986). The lack of fire in recent years is reflected by the Douglas-fir invasion into the xeric grassland located in the northwestern part of the RNA (fig 4.)

Following the 1962 Columbus Day storm, 560 windthrown trees were salvage logged and removed from the site in 1964–65. Roads associated with this logging have been subsequently abandoned and are now overgrown. At the same time, two areas totaling 6.9 ha (17 ac) were clearcut and replanted (Curtis 1986).

Grazing by domestic livestock is presumed to be the early cause for degradation of the 2.4-ha (6-ac) xeric meadow located in the northwestern part of the RNA. Today, the site is dominated by invasive, nonnative grasses, such as orchardgrass (*Dactylis glomerata*), bristly dogstail grass (*Cynosurus echinatus*), common velvetgrass (*Holcus lanatus*), and silver hairgrass (*Aira caryophyllea*) (Curtis 1986). The area is closed to off-road vehicles (USDI BLM 1995); however, there have been a few violations recently, and efforts have been made to reduce impacts by gating the area.

Research History

The following research and monitoring projects have been undertaken within the Camas Swale RNA (Greene et al.1986, USDI BLM 1982):

Brewster, J.H. 1977. Forest succession and aspects of microclimate on a south-facing slope in the BLM Camas Swale Natural Area.

Carroll, G.C.; Carroll, F.E. 1978. Studies on the incidence of coniferous needle endophytes in the Pacific Northwest.

Christy, J.A.; Alverson, E.R.; Dougherty, M.P.; Kolar, S.C.; Alton, C.W.; Hawes, S.M.; Hickman, G.; Hiebler, J.A.; Nielsen, E.M. 2009. Classification of historical vegetation in Oregon, as recorded by General Land Office surveyors.

Maser, C. 1973. A preliminary list of mammals, birds, amphibians and reptiles of proposed Camas Swale, Fox Hollow, and Mohawk Research Natural Areas.

Schuller, R.; Greene, S.; Widmer, M.; Downing, G.; Mayrsohn, C.; Curtis, A. 2001. Unpublished monitoring data.

Schuller, R.; Greene, S. 2009. Unpublished monitoring data.

Vander Schaaf, D. 1977. An examination of small stand openings in a Douglas-fir forest in the Willamette Valley foothills.

White, D. 1974. Floristic list of proposed Camas Swale, Fox Hollow, and Mohawk Research Natural Areas.

Maps

Maps applicable to Camas Swale RNA: Topographic—Creswell, Oregon, 7.5 minute, 1:24,000 scale, 1984; Eugene BLM District transportation map, 1:63,360 [no date].

Acknowledgments

The following people merit recognition for their contributions. Jay Ruegger, geographic information system specialist, created the maps in figures 1 and 2, and Dan Crannell, wildlife biologist, Eugene District, BLM, reviewed and improved the list of animals in appendix 2. We also thank the three manuscript reviewers: Todd Wilson, wildlife biologist and RNA coordinator, U.S. Forest Service, Pacific Northwest (PNW) Research Station; Nancy Sawtelle, BLM Eugene District plant ecologist, and Shami Premdas, BLM Eugene District landscape planner, for reviewing the manuscript. The project is funded through the Eugene District BLM and is administratively supported by the USDA Forest Service PNW Research Station.

English Equivalents

1 hectare (ha) = 2.47 acres (ac)
1 kilometer (km) = 0.62 mile (mi)
1 meter (m) = 3.28 feet (ft)
1 square meter (m^2) = 10.76 square feet
1 centimeter (cm) = 0.394 inch (in)
1 millimeter (mm) = 0.0394 inch
Degrees Fahrenheit (°F) = 1.8 degrees Celsius + 32

References

Baitis, K. 2010. Personal communication. Soil scientist, USDI Bureau of Land Management, P.O. Box 10226, Eugene, OR 97440-2226.

Brewster, J.H. 1977. Forest succession and aspects of microclimate on a south-facing slope in the BLM Camas Swale Natural Area. Unpublished manuscript. On file with: USDA Forest Service, Pacific Northwest Research Station, 3200 SW Jefferson Way, Corvallis, OR 97331.

Carroll, G.C.; Carroll, F.E. 1978. Studies on the incidence of coniferous needle endophytes in the Pacific Northwest. Canadian Journal of Botany. 56(24): 3034–3043.

Christy, J.A.; Alverson E.R.; Dougherty M.P.; Kolar S.C.; Alton C.W.; Hawes, S.M.; Ashkenas, L.; Minear, P. 2009. General Land Office historical vegetation of the Willamette Valley, Oregon, 1851-1910. ArcMap shapefile, Version 2009_07. Oregon Natural Heritage Information Center, Oregon State University. (September 28, 2010).

Csuti, B.; Kimerling, A.J.; O'Neil, T.A.; Shaughnessy, M.M.; Gaines, E.P.; Huso, M.M.P. 1997. Atlas of Oregon wildlife. Corvallis, OR: Oregon State University Press. 427 p. + map.

Curtis, A.B. 1986. Camas Swale Research Natural Area. Supplement to: Franklin, J.F.; Hall, F.C.; Dyrness, C.T.; Maser, C. 1972. Federal research natural areas in Oregon and Washington. Portland, OR: U.S. Department of Agriculture, Forest Service, Pacific Northwest Forest and Range Experiment Station. 18 p.

Dyrness, C.T.; Franklin, J.F.; Maser, C.; Cook, S.A.; Hall, J.D.; Faxon, G. 1975. Research natural area needs in the Pacific Northwest: a contribution to land-use planning. Gen. Tech. Rep. PNW-38. Portland, OR: U.S. Department of Agriculture, Forest Service, Pacific Northwest Forest and Range Experiment Station. 231 p.

Flora of North America. 1993+. Partial nomenclature of vascular plants, ferns, and fern allies within Oregon. http://www.efloras.org/flora_page.aspx?flora_id=1. (September 23, 2010).

Franklin, J.F.; Dyrness, C.T. 1988. 2nd ed. Natural vegetation of Oregon and Washington. Corvallis, OR: Oregon State University Press. 452 p.

Greene, S.E.; Blinn, T.; Franklin, J.F. 1986. Research natural areas in Oregon and Washington: past and current research and related literature. Gen. Tech. Rep. PNW-GTR-197. Portland, OR: U.S. Department of Agriculture, Forest Service, Pacific Northwest Research Station. 115 p.

Kovalchik, B.L.; Clausnitzer, R.R. 2004. Classification and management of aquatic, riparian, and wetland sites on the national forests of eastern Washington: series description. Gen. Tech. Rep. PNW-GTR-593. Portland, OR: U.S. Department of Agriculture, Forest Service, Pacific Northwest Research Station. 354 p. In cooperation with: Pacific Northwest Region, Colville, Okanogan, and Wenatchee National Forests.

Maser, C. 1973. A preliminary list of mammals, birds, amphibians and reptiles of proposed Camas Swale, Fox Hollow, and Mohawk Research Natural Areas. Unpublished report. On file with: U.S. Department of Agriculture, Pacific Northwest Research Station, 3200 SW Jefferson Way, Corvallis, OR 97331.

McCain, C.; Diaz, N. 2002. Field guide to the forested plant associations of the northern Oregon Coast Range. Tech. Pap. R6-NR-ECOL-TP-02-02. Portland, OR: U.S. Department of Agriculture, Forest Service, Pacific Northwest Region. 250 p.

Oregon Flora Project. 2010. The Oregon plant atlas. http://www.oregonflora.org/oregonplantatlas.html. (July 14, 2010).

Oregon Natural Heritage Program. 2003. Oregon natural heritage plan. Salem, OR: Department of State Lands. 167 p.

Patching, W.R. 1987. Soil survey of Lane County area, Oregon. Portland, OR: U.S. Department of Agriculture, Natural Resources Conservation Service. http://www.or.nrcs.usda.gov/pnw_soil/or_data.html. (September 16, 2010).

Schuller, R.; Greene, S.; 2009. Unpublished monitoring data. On file with: U.S. Department of Agriculture, Forest Service, Pacific Northwest Research Station, 3200 SW Jefferson Way. Corvallis, OR 97331.

Schuller, R.; Greene, S.; Widmer, M.; Downing, G.; Mayrsohn, C.; Curtis, A. 2001. Unpublished monitoring data. On file with: U.S. Department of Agriculture, Forest Service, Pacific Northwest Research Station, 3200 SW Jefferson Way. Corvallis, OR 97331.

U.S. Department of Agriculture, Natural Resources Conservation Service [USDA NRCS]. 2010. Soil maps from Lane County, Oregon. http://websoilsurvey.nrcs.usda.gov/app/WebSoilSurvey.aspx. (July 14, 2010).

U.S. Department of the Interior, Bureau of Land Management [USDI BLM]. 1982. Camas Swale Research Natural Area—management plan. Unpublished manuscript. On file with: Bureau of Land Management, Eugene District Office, 3106 Pierce Parkway, Suite E, Springfield, OR 97477. 12 p.

U.S. Department of the Interior, Bureau of Land Management [USDI BLM]. 1995. Record of decision and resource management plan. Springfield, OR: Eugene District. 263 p.

Vander Schaaf, D. 1977. An examination of small stand openings in a Douglas-fir forest in the Willamette Valley foothills. Unpublished report. On file with: U.S. Department of Agriculture, Forest Service, Pacific Northwest Research Station, 3200 SW Jefferson Way, Corvallis, OR 97331.

Western Region Climate Center [WRCC]. 2010. Oregon climate data. Eugene WSO Airport, Oregon (352709). Monthly climate summary 12/1/1939 to 12/31/2009. http://www.wrcc.dri.edu/cgi-bin/cliMAIN.pl?or2709. (May 31, 2010).

White, D. 1974. Floristic list of proposed Camas Swale, Fox Hollow, and Mohawk Research Natural Areas. Unpublished manuscript. On file with: U.S. Department of Agriculture, Forest Service, Pacific Northwest Research Station, 3200 SW Jefferson Way, Corvallis, OR 97331.

Wilson, T.M.; Schuller, R.; Holmes, R.; Pavola, C.; Fimbel, R.A.; McCain, C.N.; Gamon, J.G.; Speaks, P.; Seevers, J.I.; DeMeo, T.E.; Gibbons, S. 2009. Interagency strategy for the Pacific Northwest Natural Areas Network. Gen. Tech. Rep. PNW-GTR-798. Portland, OR: U.S. Department of Agriculture, Forest Service, Pacific Northwest Research Station. 33 p.

Appendix 1: Plants[1] [2]

Scientific name	Common name

Coniferous trees:

Abies grandis (Dougl.) Forbes	Grand fir
Calocedrus decurrens (Torr.) Florin	Incense cedar
Pinus ponderosa Dougl.	Ponderosa pine
Pseudotsuga menziesii (Mirbel) Franco	Douglas-fir
Taxus brevifolia Nutt.	Western yew
Thuja plicata Donn ex D. Don	Western redcedar
Tsuga heterophylla (Raf.) Sarg.	Western hemlock

Deciduous trees >8 m (26.3 ft) tall:

Acer macrophyllum Pursh	Bigleaf maple
Alnus rubra Bong.	Red alder
Arbutus menziesii Pursh	Pacific madrone
Chrysolepis chrysophylla (Dougl. ex Hook.) Hjelmq.	Giant chinquapin
Cornus nuttallii Aud. ex T. & G.	Pacific dogwood
Fraxinus latifolia Benth.	Oregon ash
Prunus emarginata (Dougl. ex Hook.) D. Dietr.	Bitter cherry
Quercus garryana Dougl.	Oregon white oak

Tall shrubs 2 to 8 m (6.6 to 26.3 ft) tall:

Acer circinatum Pursh	Vine maple
Amelanchier alnifolia Nutt.	Western serviceberry
Corylus cornuta Marsh. var. *californica* (DC.) Sharp	Hazelnut
Holodiscus discolor (Pursh) Maxim.	Oceanspray
Philadelphus lewisii Pursh	Lewis' mock orange
Rhamnus purshiana DC.	Cascara
Rhododendron macrophyllum D. Don ex G. Don	Pacific rhododendron
Salix scouleriana Barratt ex Hook.	Scouler's willow
Sambucus nigra L. ssp. *cerulea* (Raf.) Bolli	Blue elderberry
Sambucus racemosa L. var. *arborescens* (T. & G) Gray	Red elderberry

Medium shrubs 0.5 to 2 m (1.6 to 6.6 ft) tall:

Berberis aquifolium Pursh	Tall Oregongrape
Ceanothus velutinus Dougl.	Sticky laurel
Gaultheria shallon Pursh	Salal
Lonicera hispidula (Lindl.) Dougl. ex T. & G.	Pink honeysuckle
Rosa gymnocarpa Nutt.	Baldhip rose
Rubus laciniatus Willd.	Cutleaf blackberry
Rubus leucodermis Dougl. ex T. & G.	Whitebark raspberry
Rubus parviflorus Nutt.	Thimbleberry
Symphoricarpos albus (L.) Blake	Common snowberry

Symphoricarpos mollis Nutt.	Creeping snowberry
Toxicodendron diversilobum (T. & G.) Greene	Poison oak
Vaccinium parvifolium Sm.	Red huckleberry
Viburnum ellipticum Hook.	Common viburnum

Low shrubs <0.5 m (1.6 ft) tall:

Berberis nervosa Pursh	Oregongrape
Rubus ursinus Cham. & Schlecht.	California blackberry
Whipplea modesta Torr.	Whipplevine

Ferns and allies:

Adiantum pedatum L.	Maidenhair fern
Athyrium filix-femina (L.) Roth.	Lady fern
Dryopteris arguta (Kaulf.) Watt.	Coastal wood fern
Pityrogramma triangularis (Kaulf.) Maxon	Goldfern
Polypodium glycyrrhiza DC. Eat.	Licorice fern
Polystichum munitum (Kaulf.) Presl	Western swordfern
Pteridium aquilinum (L.) Kuhn.	Bracken fern

Herbs:

Achillea millefolium L.	Common yarrow
Achlys californica I. Fukuda & H.G. Baker	Deer's foot
Achlys triphylla (Sm.) DC.	Sweet after death
Adenocaulon bicolor Hook.	American trailplant
Anaphalis margaritacea (L.) B. & H.	Pearly everlasting
Anemone deltoidea Hook.	Columbian windflower
Angelica arguta Nutt.	Lyall's angelica
Angelica genuflexa Nutt.	Kneeling angelica
Anisocarpus madioides Nutt.	Woodland madia
Aquilegia formosa Fisch.	Red columbine
Asarum caudatum Lindl.	Wild ginger
Athysanus pusillus (Hook.) Greene	Common sandweed
Brodiaea sp.	Brodiaea
Calochortus tolmiei H. & A.	Tolmie star tulip
Calycadenia truncata DC.	Oregon western rosinweed
Calypso bulbosa (L.) Oakes	Fairy slipper
Campanula prenanthoides (Dur.) McVaugh	California harebell
Cardamine oligosperma Nutt. in T. & G.	Little western bittercress
Cardamine nuttallii Greene var. *nuttallii*	Palmate toothwort
Centaurium erythraea Rafn.	European centaury
Cerastium arvense L.	Field chickweed
Cerastium viscosum L.	Sticky chickweed
Cerastium vulgatum L.	Common chickweed
Chamerion angustifolium (L.) Holub ssp. *circumvagum* (Mosq.) Hoch	Fireweed
Chimaphila umbellata (L.) Bart. ssp. *umbellata*	Pipsissewa
Circaea alpina L.	Alpine circaea
Cirsium arvense (L.) Scop. var. *horridum* Wimm. & Grab.	Canada thistle

Cirsium vulgare (Savi) Ten.	Bull thistle
Claytonia parviflora Dougl. ex Hook. ssp. *parviflora*	Streambank springbeauty
Claytonia sibirica L.	Siberian springbeauty
Collinsia grandiflora Lindl.	Large-flowered blue-eyed Mary
Collinsia parviflora Lindl.	Small-flowered blue-eyed Mary
Collomia heterophylla Hook.	Varied-leaf collomia
Comandra umbellata (L.) Nutt.	Bastard toadflax
Coptis laciniata Gray	Cutleaf goldthread
Corallorhiza mertensiana Bong.	Pacific coralroot
Corallorhiza striata Lindl.	Hooded coralroot
Cynoglossum grande Dougl. ex Lehm	Pacific hound's-tongue
Daucus carota L.	Queen Anne's lace
Dodecatheon hendersonii Gray	Henderson's shooting star
Draba verna L.	Spring whitlow-grass
Epilobium brachycarpum C. Presl	Tall annual willowherb
Equisetum telmateia Ehrh.	Giant horsetail
Eriophyllum lanatum (Pursh) Forbes	Common woolly sunflower
Erodium cicutarium (L.) L'Her.	Stork's bill
Erythronium oregonum Appleg.	Giant white fawn lily
Fragaria vesca L.	Woodland strawberry
Fritillaria affinis (Schult.) Sealy var. *affinis*	Checker lily
Galium aparine L.	Stickywilly
Galium triflorum Michx.	Sweet-scented bedstraw
Geranium dissectum L.	Cutleaf geranium
Geranium molle L.	Dovefoot geranium
Goodyera oblongifolia Raf.	Western rattlesnake plantain
Hypericum perforatum L.	St. John's wort
Hypochaeris radicata L.	Hairy cat's-ear
Inula helenium L.	Elecampane inula
Iris chrysophylla Howell	Yellow leaf iris
Iris tenax Dougl. ex Lindl.	Toughleaf iris
Lathyrus pauciflorus Fern.	Few-flower peavine
Lathyrus polyphyllus Nutt.	Leafy peavine
Leucanthemum vulgare Lam.	Oxeye daisy
Ligusticum apiifolium (Nutt. ex T. & G.) Gray	Celeryleaf licoraceroot
Linnaea borealis L.	Twinflower
Lithophragma parviflorum (Hook.) Nutt.	Smallflower woodlandstar
Lomatium utriculatum (Nutt.) Coult. & Rose	Common lomatium
Lotus sp.	Deervetch
Madia gracilis (Sm.) Keck	Grassy tarweed
Maianthemum stellatum (L.) Desf.	Starry false-Solomonseal
Marah oreganus (T. & G.) Howell	Wild cucumber
Microsteris gracilis (Hook.) Greene var. *gracilis*	Pink microsteris
Mimulus alsinoides Dougl. ex Benth.	Wingstem monkeyflower
Mimulus guttatus DC.	Common monkeyflower
Mimulus moschatus Dougl.	Musk flower
Minuartia cismontana R.J. Meinke & P.F. Zika	Cismontane minuartia

Moehringia macrophylla (Hook.) Fenzl	Largeleaf sandwort
Myosotis discolor Pers.	Yellow and blue forget-me-not
Myosotis laxa Lehm.	Small flowered forget-me-not
Navarretia intertexta (Benth.) Hook.	Needleleaf navarretia
Nemophila menziesii H. & A.	Baby blue eyes
Nemophila parviflora Dougl. ex Benth.	Small-flowered nemophila
Orobanche uniflora L.	Oneflowered broomerape
Osmorhiza berteroi DC.	Sweetcicely
Oxalis suksdorfii Trel.	Suksdorf woodsorrel
Perideridia gairdneri (H. & A.) Math.	Gairdner's yampah
Plantago lanceolata L.	English plantain
Polygonum douglasii Greene	Douglas' knotweed
Potentilla gracilis Dougl. ex Hook. var. *gracilis*	Slender cinquefoil
Prunella vulgaris L. spp. *vulgaris*	Self heal
Ranunculus occidentalis Nutt. var. *occidentalis*	Western buttercup
Ranunculus uncinatus D. Don ex G. Don	Woodland buttercup
Rudbeckia occidentalis L.	Western coneflower
Rumex acetosella L.	Common sheep sorrel
Sanicula crassicaulis Poepp.	Pacific blacksnakeroot
Satureja douglasii (Benth.) Briq.	Yerba buena
Saxifraga oregana Howell	Oregon saxifrage
Senecio jacobaea L.	Tansy ragwort
Stachys rigida Nutt. ex Benth.	Rough hedgenettle
Stellaria crispa Cham. & Schlecht.	Curled starwort
Synthyris reniformis (Dougl. ex Benth.) Benth.	Snowqueen
Thermopsis gracilis Howell var. *gracilis*	Slender goldenbanner
Tiarella trifoliata L. var. unifoliata (Hook.) Kurtz	Oneleaf foamflower
Tonella tenella (Benth.) Heller	Lesser baby innocence
Torilis arvensis (Huds.) Link	Spreading hedge parsley
Trientalis borealis Raf. ssp. *latifolia* (Hook.) Hultén	Broadleaf starflower
Trifolium variegatum Nutt.	Whitetip clover
Vancouveria hexandra (Hook.) Morr. & Dec.	Inside-out flower
Veronica arvensis L.	Corn speedwell
Vicia americana Muhl. ex Willd.	American vetch
Viola sempervirens Greene	Evergreen violet

Grasses, sedges and rushes:

Agrostis hallii Vasey	Hall's bentgrass
Aira caryophyllea L.	Silver hairgrass
Bromus hordeaceus L.	Soft brome
Bromus vulgaris (Hook.) Shear	Common brome
Cynosurus echinatus L.	Bristly dogstail grass
Dactylis glomerata L.	Orchardgrass
Elymus glaucus Buckl.	Blue wildrye
Elymus multisetus (Sm.) Burtt Davy	Big squirreltail
Festuca californica Vasey	California fescue

Festuca occidentalis Hook.	Western fescue
Festuca subulata Trin.	Bearded fescue
Holcus lanatus L.	Common velvetgrass
Juncus sp.	Rush
Luzula multiflora (Ehrh.) Lej. ssp. *multiflora*	Common woodrush
Melica subulata (Griseb.) Scribn.	Alaska oniongrass
Poa annua L.	Annual bluegrass
Poa trivialis L.	Roughstalk bluegrass
Scirpus microcarpus J. Presl & C. Presl.	Panicled bulrush
Vulpia microstachys (Nutt.) Munro	Small fescue

[1] Nomenclature for vascular plants, ferns, and fern-allies follows Flora of North America (1993+) and the Oregon Flora Project Web site (2010).

[2] Compiled from field surveys (Curtis 1986, White 1974) with additions in recent years.

Appendix 2: Amphibians, Reptiles, Birds, and Mammals[1][2]

Family	Scientific name	Common name
Amphibians:		
Ambystomatidae	*Ambystoma gracile*	Northwestern salamander
	Ambystoma macrodactylum	Long-toed salamander
Dicamptodontidae	*Dicamptodon tenebrosus*	Pacific giant salamander
Plethodontidae	*Aneides ferreus*	Clouded salamander
	Ensatina eschscholtzii	Ensatina
	Plethodon dunni	Dunn's salamander
	Plethodon vehiculum	Western redback
Salamandridae	*Taricha granulosa*	Roughskin newt
Bufonidae	*Bufo boreas*	Western toad
Hylidae	*Pseudacris regilla*	Pacific chorus frog
Ranidae	*Rana aurora*	Red-legged frog
Reptiles:		
Anguidae	*Elgaria coerulea*	Northern alligator lizard
	Elgaria multicarinata	Southern alligator lizard
Scincidae	*Eumeces skiltonianus*	Western skink
Boidae	*Charina bottae*	Rubber boa
Colubridae	*Coluber constrictor*	Racer
	Contia tenuis	Sharptail snake
	Diadophis punctatus	Ringneck snake
	Pituophis catenifer	Gopher snake
	Thamnophis elegans	Western terrestrial garter snake
	Thamnophis ordinoides	Northwestern garter snake
	Thamnophis sirtalis	Common garter snake
Iguanidae	*Sceloporus occidentalis*	Western fence lizard
Viperidae	*Crotalus oreganus*	Northern Pacific rattlesnake
Birds:		
Cathartidae	*Cathartes aura*	Turkey vulture
Accipitridae	*Accipiter gentilis*	Northern goshawk
	Accipiter striatus	Sharp-shinned hawk
	Accipiter cooperii	Cooper's hawk
	Buteo jamaicensis	Red-tailed hawk
Falconidae	*Falco sparverius*	American kestrel
Phasianidae	*Bonasa umbellus*	Ruffed grouse
	Callipepla californica	California quail
	Dendragapus obscurus	Blue grouse
	Meleagris gallopavo	Wild turkey
	Oreortyx pictus	Mountain quail
	Phasianus colchicus	Ring-necked pheasant
Charadriidae	*Charadrius vociferus*	Killdeer
Scolopacidae	*Actitis macularia*	Spotted sandpiper
Columbidae	*Columba fasciata*	Band-tailed pigeon
	Zenaida macroura	Mourning dove

Strigidae	*Otus kennicottii*	Western screech-owl
	Bubo virginianus	Great-horned owl
	Glaucidium gnoma	Northern pygmy-owl
	Strix occidentalis	Spotted owl
	Strix varia	Barred owl
	Aegolius acadicus	Northern saw-whet owl
Caprimulgidae	*Chordeiles minor*	Common nighthawk
Apodidae	*Chaetura vauxi*	Vaux's swift
Trochilidae	*Calypte anna*	Anna's hummingbird
	Selasphorus rufus	Rufous hummingbird
Picidae	*Sphyrapicus ruber*	Red-breasted sapsucker
	Picoides pubescens	Downy woodpecker
	Picoides villosus	Hairy woodpecker
	Colaptes auratus	Northern flicker
	Dryocopus pileatus	Pileated woodpecker
Tyrannidae	*Contopus borealis*	Olive-sided flycatcher
	Contopus sordidulus	Western wood peewee
	Empidonax hammondii	Hammond's flycatcher
	Empidonax traillii	Willow flycatcher
	Empidonax difficilis	Pacific-slope flycatcher
	Tyrannus verticalis	Western kingbird
Hirundinidae	*Hirundo pyrrhonota*	Cliff swallow
	Hirundo rustica	Barn swallow
	Progne subis	Purple martin
	Tachycineta bicolor	Tree swallow
	Tachycineta thalassina	Violet-green swallow
Corvidae	*Perisoreus canadensis*	Gray jay
	Cyanocitta stelleri	Steller's jay
	Corvus brachyrhynchos	American crow
	Corvus corax	Common raven
Paridae	*Parus atricapillus*	Black-capped chickadee
	Parus rufescens	Chestnut-backed chickadee
Aegithalidae	*Psaltriparus minimus*	Bushtit
Sittidae	*Sitta canadensis*	Red-breasted nuthatch
	Sitta caroliniensis	White-breasted nuthatch
Certhiidae	*Certhia americana*	Brown creeper
Troglodytidae	*Thryomanes bewickii*	Bewick's wren
	Troglodytes aedon	House wren
	Troglodytes troglodytes	Winter wren
Muscicapidae	*Chamaea fasciata*	Wrentit
	Catharus guttatus	Hermit thrush
	Catharus ustulatus	Swainson's thrush
	Ixoreus naevius	Varied thrush
	Myadestes townsendi	Townsend's solitaire
	Regulus satrapa	Golden-crowned kinglet
	Sialia mexicana	Western bluebird
	Turdus migratorius	American robin
Bombycillidae	*Bombycilla cedrorum*	Cedar waxwing
Vireonidae	*Vireo cassinii*	Cassin's vireo
	Vireo gilvus	Warbling vireo
	Vireo huttoni	Hutton's vireo

Emberizidae	*Dendroica coronata*	Yellow-rumped warbler
	Dendroica petechia	Yellow warbler
	Dendroica nigrescens	Black-throated gray warbler
	Dendroica occidentalis	Hermit warbler
	Junco hyemalis	Dark-eyed junco
	Melospiza melodia	Song sparrow
	Molothrus ater	Brown-headed cowbird
	Oporornis tolmiei	MacGillivray's warbler
	Passerella iliaca	Fox sparrow
	Pheucticus melanocephalus	Black-headed grosbeak
	Pipilo maculatus	Spotted towhee
	Piranga rubra	Western tanager
	Spizella passerina	Chipping sparrow
	Wilsonia pusilla	Wilson's warbler
	Zonotrichia atricapilla	Golden-crowned sparrow
	Zonotrichia leucophrys	White-crowned sparrow
Fringillidae	*Carduelis pinus*	Pine siskin
	Carduelis psaltria	Lesser goldfinch
	Carduelis tristis	American goldfinch
	Coccothraustes vespertinus	Evening grosbeak
	Loxia curvirostra	Red crossbill

Mammals:

Didelphidae	*Didelphis virginiana*	Virginia opossum
Soricidae	*Sorex sonomae*	Fog shrew
	Sorex pacificus	Pacific shrew
	Sorex bendirii	Pacific marsh shrew
	Sorex trowbridgii	Trowbridge's shrew
Talpidae	*Neurotrichus gibbsii*	Shrew-mole
	Scapanus orarius	Coast mole
Vespertilionidae	*Myotis volans*	Long-legged myotis
	Myotis thysanodes	Fringed myotis
	Myotis evotis	Long-eared myotis
	Lasionycteris noctivagans	Silver-haired bat
	Eptesicus fuscus	Big brown bat
Leporidae	*Sylvilagus bachmani*	Brush rabbit
Sciuridae	*Tamias townsendii*	Townsend's chipmunk
	Sciurus griseus	Western gray squirrel
	Tamiasciurus douglasii	Douglas' squirrel
	Glaucomys sabrinus	Northern flying squirrel
Muridae	*Peromyscus maniculatus*	Deer mouse
	Neotoma fuscipes	Dusky-footed woodrat
	Neotoma cinerea	Bushy-tailed woodrat
	Clethrionomys californicus	Western red-backed vole
	Phenacomys albipes	White-footed vole
	Phenacomys longicaudus	Red tree vole
	Microtus longicaudus	Long-tailed vole
	Microtus oregoni	Creeping vole
Dipodidae	*Zapus trinotatus*	Pacific jumping mouse
Erethizontidae	*Erethizon dorsatum*	Common porcupine
Canidae	*Canis latrans*	Coyote

	Urocyon cinereoargenteus	Common gray fox
	Vulpes vulpes	Red fox
Ursidae	*Ursus americanus*	Black bear
Procyonidae	*Procyon lotor*	Common raccoon
Mustelidae	*Martes americana*	American marten
	Mustela erminea	Ermine
	Mustela frenata	Long-tailed weasel
	Spilogale gracilis	Western spotted skunk
	Mephitis mephitis	Striped skunk
Felidae	*Felis concolor*	Mountain lion
	Lynx rufus	Bobcat
Cervidae	*Cervus elaphus*	Elk
	Odocoileus hemionus ssp. *columbianus*	Black-tailed deer

[1] Compiled from field observations (Curtis 1986, Maser 1973), and from habitat descriptions and distribution maps in Csuti et al. 1997.

[2] Nomenclature taken from Csuti et al. 1997.